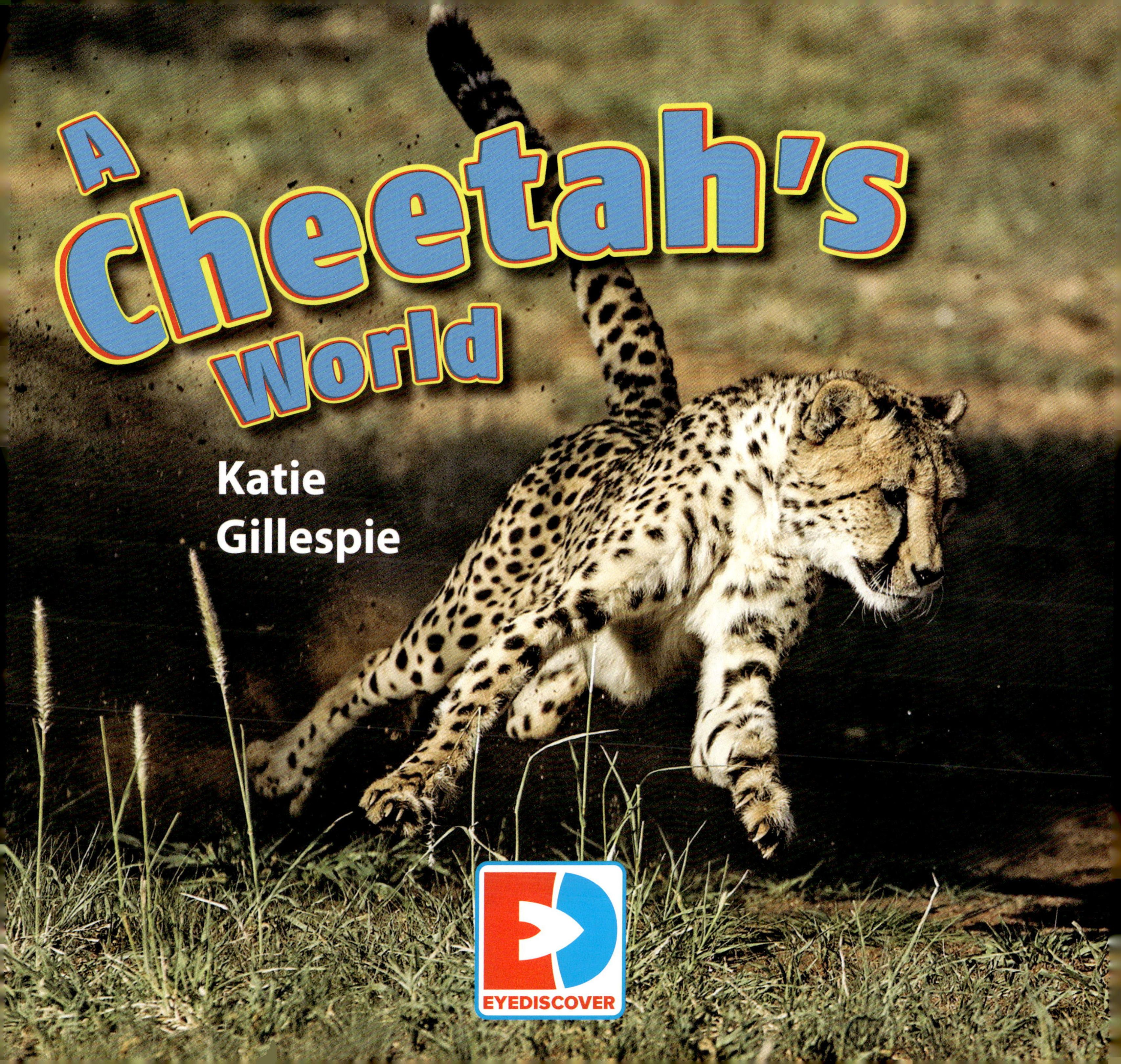
A Cheetah's World
Katie Gillespie
EYEDISCOVER

Go to **www.eyediscover.com** and enter this book's unique code.

BOOK CODE

H328985

EYEDISCOVER brings you optic readalongs that support active learning.

Published by AV² by Weigl
350 5th Avenue, 59th Floor New York, NY 10118
Website: www.eyediscover.com

Library of Congress Control Number: 2017930610

ISBN 978-1-4896-5644-5 (hardcover)

Printed in the United States of America
in Brainerd, Minnesota
1 2 3 4 5 6 7 8 9 0 21 20 19 18 17

022017
020317

Editor: Katie Gillespie
Designer: Mandy Christiansen

Weigl acknowledges Getty Images, iStock, and Shutterstock as the primary image suppliers for this title.

EYEDISCOVER provides enriched content, optimized for tablet use, that supplements and complements this book. EYEDISCOVER books strive to create inspired learning and engage young minds in a total learning experience.

Watch
Video content brings each page to life.

Browse
Thumbnails make navigation simple.

Read
Follow along with text on the screen.

Listen
Hear each page read aloud.

Your EYEDISCOVER Optic Readalongs come alive with...

Audio
Listen to the entire book read aloud.

Video
High resolution videos turn each spread into an optic readalong.

OPTIMIZED FOR
- TABLETS
- WHITEBOARDS
- COMPUTERS
- AND MUCH MORE!

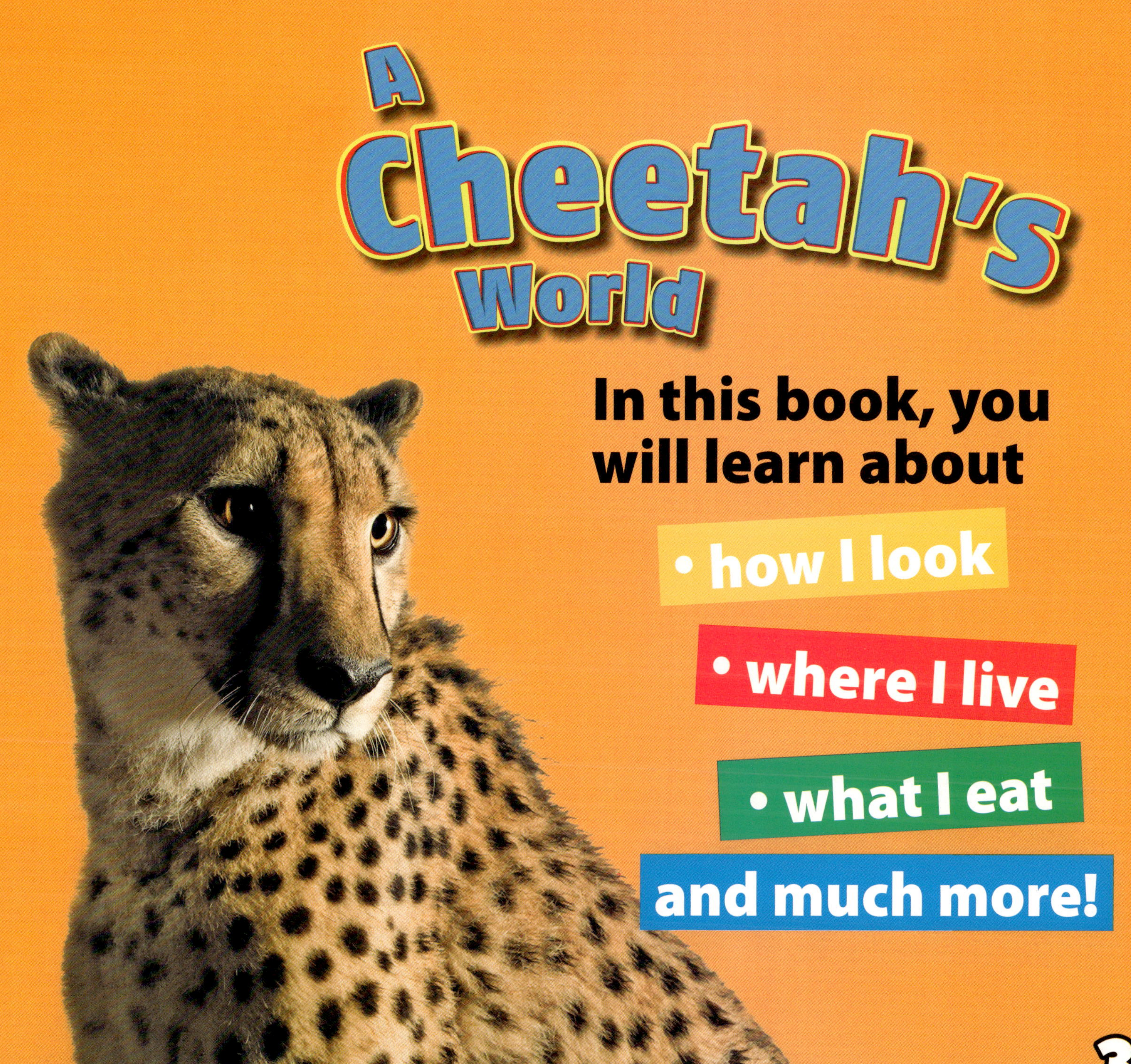

A Cheetah's World

In this book, you will learn about

- how I look
- where I live
- what I eat

and much more!

I am a cheetah.

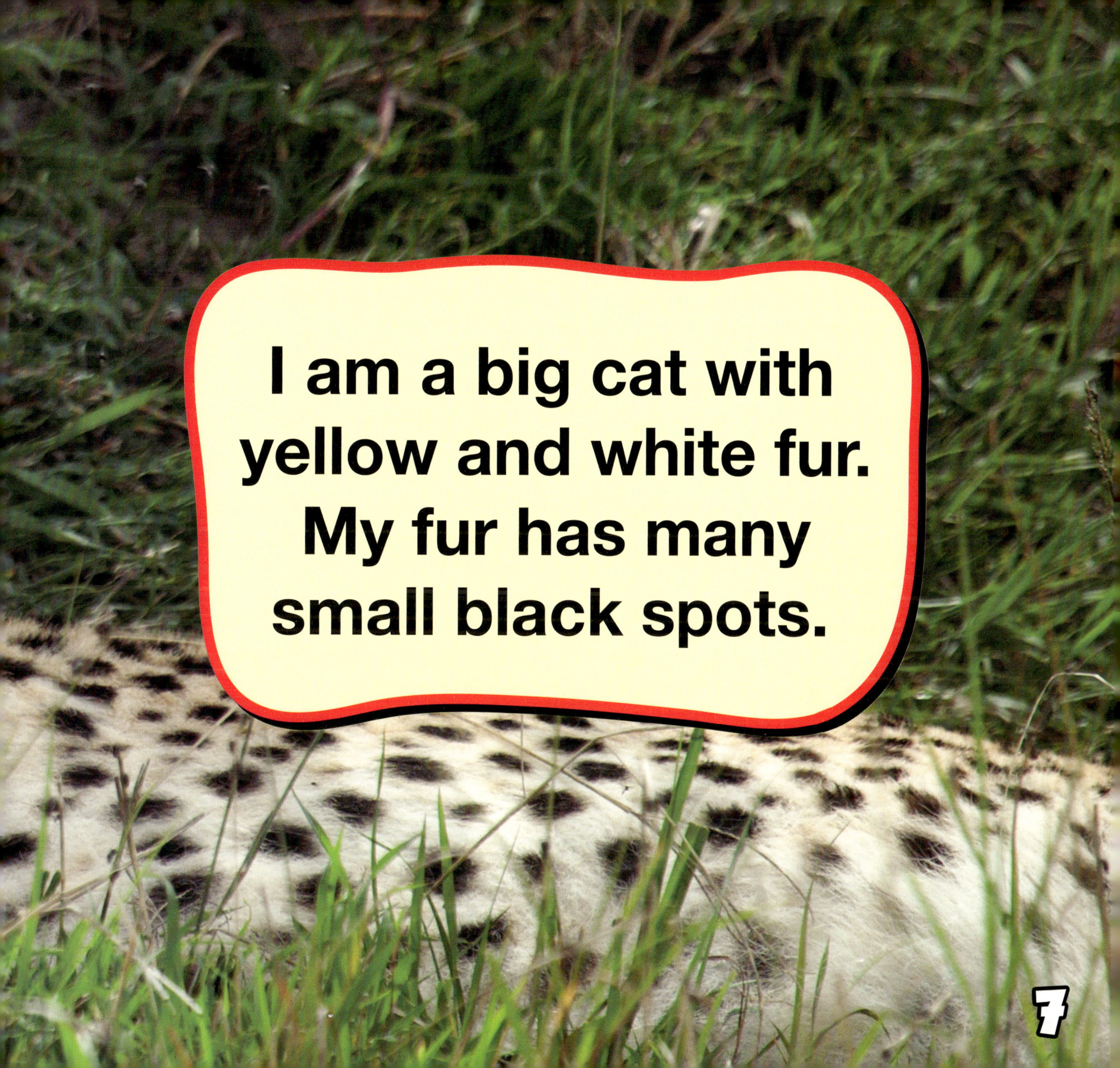

I am a big cat with yellow and white fur. My fur has many small black spots.

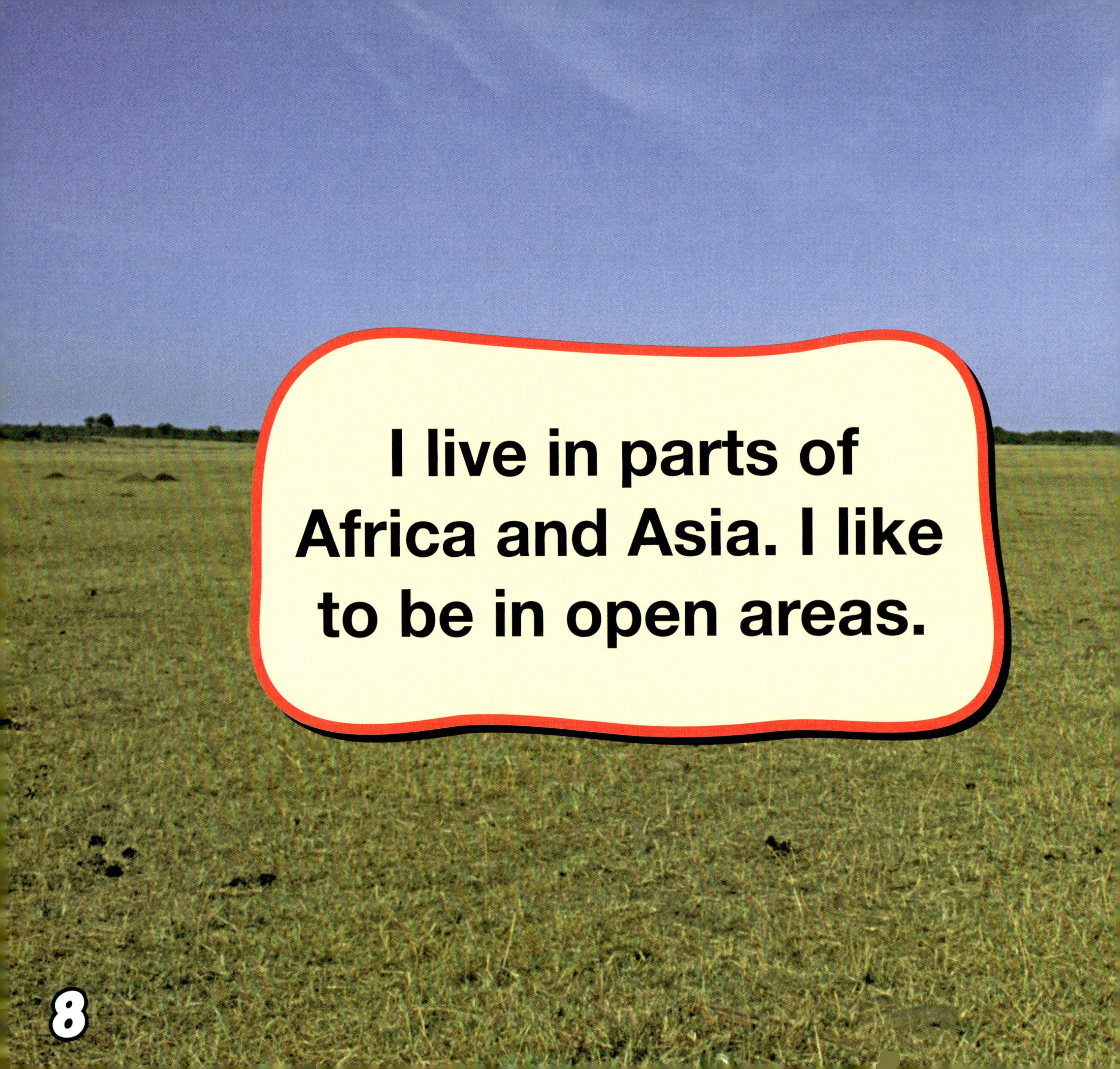

I live in parts of Africa and Asia. I like to be in open areas.

I have two black tear marks on my face. They help block sunlight so I can see better.

My body is built for speed. I am the fastest animal that lives on land.

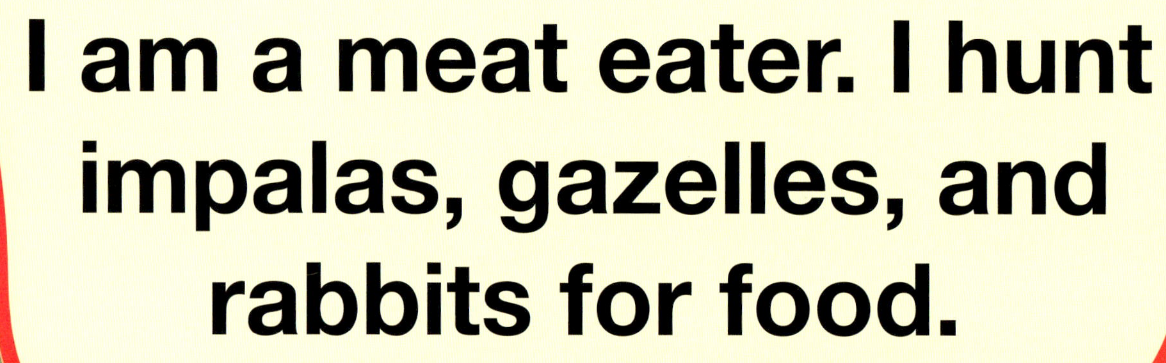
I am a meat eater. I hunt impalas, gazelles, and rabbits for food.

My strong tail has a flat shape. It helps me make quick turns while I am running.

I am not able to roar. I purr when I am happy and hiss when danger is near.

I need plenty of space to stay happy and healthy.

CHEETAHS BY THE NUMBERS

Only about **7,100 cheetahs** are left in **nature**.

It only takes **three seconds** for a cheetah to reach its top speed of **60 miles per hour.** (100 kilometers per hour)

A cheetah cub's **eyes open** within its **first 10 days.**

Mother cheetahs raise their cubs for up to **two years**.

The **largest** cheetah population **on Earth** is in **Namibia**, **Africa**. **90 %** of these cheetahs live on **farmland**.

Namibia

A cheetah has to **rest** for **30 minutes** to catch its breath **after chasing prey**.

KEY WORDS

Research has shown that as much as 65 percent of all written material published in English is made up of 300 words. These 300 words cannot be taught using pictures or learned by sounding them out. They must be recognized by sight. This book contains 44 common sight words to help young readers improve their reading fluency and comprehension. This book also teaches young readers several important content words, such as proper nouns. These words are paired with pictures to aid in learning and improve understanding.

Page	Sight Words First Appearance
4	a, am, I
7	and, big, has, many, my, small, white, with
8	be, in, like, live, of, open, parts, to
11	can, face, have, help, on, see, so, they, two
12	animal, for, is, land, that, the
14	food
17	it, make, me, turns, while
19	near, not, when
20	need

Page	Content Words First Appearance
4	cheetah
7	cat, fur, spots
8	Africa, areas, Asia
11	sunlight, tear marks
12	body, speed
14	gazelles, impalas, meat eater, rabbits
17	shape, tail
19	danger
20	space

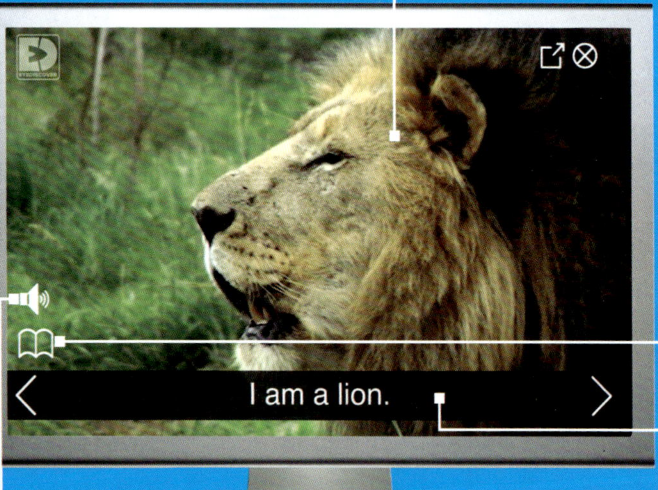

Watch
Video content brings each page to life.

Browse
Thumbnails make navigation simple.

Read
Follow along with text on the screen.

Listen
Hear each page read aloud.

Go to www.eyediscover.com and enter this book's unique code.

BOOK CODE

H328985